The Pact

The Pact

The Spiritual Friendship between
Chiara Lubich and Imam W. D. Mohammed

Roberto Catalano

Foreword by
Imam Mikal Saahir

Afterword by
Kate O'Brien and
the NextNow Group

NCP
NEW CITY PRESS
Enkindling the Spirit of Unity

Published in the United States by New City Press
136 Madison Avenue, Floors 5 & 6,
PMB #4290 New York, NY 10016
www.newcitypress.com
© 2024 New City Press (English translation)

Translated by the New City Press editorial staff
from the original Italian, "Un patto di fraternità.
L'amicizia spirituale fra Chiara Lubich e l'Imam
W.D. Mohammad," chapter 4 in Roberto Catalano,
FRATERNITÀ E DIALOGO TRA LE RELIGIONI:
Esperienze di Chiara Lubich, Citta' Nuova, Rome 2022.

Cover photo © Marcello Casubolo, CSC Audiovisivi.

Layout: Miguel Tejerina, Gary Brandl.

ISBN: 978-1-56548-589-1 (Paperback)
ISBN: 978-1-56548-590-7 (E-book)

Library of Congress Control Number: 2024931156

3rd printing: March 2025, with corrections

Printed in the United States of America

Contents

Foreword 7

A Spiritual Friendship 13

Islam in North America 14
African American Muslims,
    Elijah Muhammad, and the Nation of Islam 17
Imam Warith Deen Mohammed 18
Chiara Lubich: A Life for Unity..25
The Beginnings in Trent 26
"Apostles of Dialogue"..33

Chiara Lubich and Imam W. D. Mohammed:
    Together for Universal Brotherhood 37

The Risk of Dialogue: Toward Encounter 38
The Meeting: A Page of History 39
The Pact for Universal Brotherhood 46
The Consequences:
    Collaboration between Muslims and Christians 48
Effects and Fruits of Dialogue between
    Christians and African American Muslims................53
Experiencing God's Presence 54

Deepening of One's Faith...54
Social Consequences:
    Ethnic-religious Integration 55
The Sense of Belonging to a Single Family....................56
Conclusion:
    The Mysterious Action of the Spirit of God..............58

Afterword

"This Pact is Made Forever"...61

Appendix

"Unity in the Focolare Movement"
    (Chiara Lubich)..71

Response by Imam W. D. Mohammed 87

Notes 93

Foreword

By Imam Mikal Saahir
Nur-Allah Islamic Center, Indianapolis, Indiana

Regardless of the many challenges humanity faces, the twenty-first century, due to better and faster means of communication and much-improved means of travel, continues to witness the unifying—or some may argue, the reunifying—of the human family. A unity that is blossoming not only in secluded or isolated religious, cultural, and ethnic sectors, but more importantly these myriad communities are intersecting and coalescing around their common goodness while simultaneously highlighting and celebrating the uniqueness of the other. This coming together of humankind is possible because, more and more, humanity is properly identifying with the disciplines of mutual respect, a respect that is often accompanied by a beaming love for G_d.

Roberto Catalano has witnessed firsthand the birth and evolution of a religious-cultural-ethnic encounter of what seemed—at least on the surface—an "unlikely pair" of two leaders: one leader Christian and the other Islamic. Beginning with their respective histories, Roberto captures in print that which has captured the hearts and minds of millions of people who love and respect these two world leaders: Chiara Lubich, the founder of the Focolare Movement, and Imam W. Deen Mohammed, who led the Muslim American community for thirty-three years. In 1997 these two leaders, exemplifying powerful faith in G_d and goodness, formed a pact, a spiritual friendship that has surpassed their earthly journey. Both Chiara and Imam Mohammed passed in 2008, in March and October, respectively.

Catalano's *The Pact* illustrates the historical evolution of the societies that produced a Chiara Lubich in Italy and a W. Deen Mohammed in the United States of America. Chiara and W. Deen were both born in challenging circumstances that, through the mercy of G_d, brought out the best in them. Within their respective life experiences each leader searched for that which they believed G_d wanted them to see, understand, and pursue.

W. Deen's father, the Honorable Elijah Muhammad, had taken a Black nationalistic approach to solving the American Blacks' problems. Albeit called "Islam," Elijah Muhammad's Nation of Islam message in many ways went against the grain of the Qur'an; however, this dichotomy challenged W. Deen's mind to work his way out of his father's Black Nationalist presentation of religion, a necessary journey that led him to embrace the universal teachings of Al-Islam, proper. Imam Mohammed's Nation of Islam experience as clarified by the Qur'an and the Prophet Muhammad (of Arabia) produced a new world leadership for humanity.

Chiara, too, blossomed from challenging surroundings. World War II came directly to her neighborhood, bringing despair and devastation; ironically, this difficult environment provided a unique opportunity to shield her life with scripture, prayer, and action. She and her close companions rose up to face the task presented before them. The phrase *Omnia vincit amor*, "love conquers all," was birthed out of her anguish. Through the trials of World War II G_d imbued Chiara with special insightful lessons that carried her life and mission forward and bestowed upon her a vision and leadership that today has reached the world.

The Qur'an reminds humanity, "We made you tribes and nations so that you would get acquainted with and recognize each other." This "spiritual friendship" formed by Chiara and Imam W. Deen is a true expression of this Qur'anic verse, which encourages people from diverse backgrounds to "get acquainted with and recognize each other" (Quran 49:13). This mutual recognizing of the other gives a firm foundation, as Catalano points out, for sincere unity and an answer to Christ Jesus' prayer, "May they all be one" (John 17:21).

A "spiritual friendship" is where souls connect; the original soul as created by G_d and undefiled by worldly concerns. Catalano shows how such a relationship, a spiritual friendship, transcends race, gender, culture, or national origin, thus becoming a stabilizing anchor and a beacon of light that, along with uniting two communities, also serves as a model of natural unity for our human family.

Catalano shares with the reader how Imam W. Deen's and Lady Chiara's spiritual friendship continues to build tangible results and relationships that disassemble the many unnatural man-made barriers that hinder human progress. While recognizing that early on some viewed such a spiritual friendship as "risky," Catalano demonstrates how the two visionary leaders understood that our diversity is our strength. Imam W. Deen, speaking in Harlem at the famous Malcolm Shabazz Mosque in May of 1997, shared, "and G_d has made things different, and human beings too, different, because he wants that unity to progress. The diversity is to provide the unity with legs, with wheels, with movement, so that we can have more movement and more progress." Lady Chiara's statement resonates with W. Deen's words. Speaking in Washington, DC, in November of 2000, she shared, "I am sure that Allah was pleased, seeing so many of his children, although different in origin, nation, religion, so united in him. And who knows what blessings he has in store for all of us who have become brothers and sisters!"

Myself, a longtime student of Imam W. Deen Mohammed and a more recent new student of Lady Chiara Lubich, I have traveled to many cities in America as well as numerous cities in Italy, the Philippines, and Jordan, receiving and processing myriad messages and examples of universal brotherhood. I'm grateful for the blessed opportunity to be a firsthand witness to the formation and fruition of a miracle of G_d's love for the human family in that He permitted a twenty-first-century model of the unity of mankind to manifest itself for all to see.

World leaders from Judaism, Islam, Christianity, Buddhism, and other faith traditions have recognized the spiritual friendship that has been established between Imam Mohammed and Chiara Lubich, a friendship that continues to serve as a testimony of tomorrow's hope.

The work begun by Chiara Lubich and Imam W. Deen Mohammed, in shaa Allah (G_d willing), is not near completion. In fact, we believe that it is just beginning. Roberto Catalano has captured an important moment that comes along rarely within our histories. It is a demonstration of faith in positive outgrowths from a newfound unity that many new spiritual friends believe has an outstanding future not only for the individuals and communities highlighted in his *The Pact*, but also an outstanding future for all of humanity.

A Spiritual Friendship

By Roberto Catalano

In March 2014, on the occasion of a conference in memory of Chiara Lubich, held at the Aula Magna of the Pontifical Urbaniana University in Rome, Imam Ronald Shaheed of Milwaukee concluded his speech by underlining the originality of the experience of interreligious dialogue born from the relationship between Chiara Lubich and the Focolare Movement she founded, and Imam Warith Deen Mohammed with the community of Muslims who support his ministry. "[It can] represent a model for the whole world," he said. "I believe that God and only God could have made it possible."[1] A few weeks later, African American Muslim judge David A. Shaheed of Indianapolis[2] returned to the same subject and, referring to the experience of dialogue between the Focolare and African American Muslims, spoke of an extraordinary collaboration with a unique spiritual dimension.

> [It goes] against any common logic that the son of the leader [of the Nation of Islam] would begin a close collaboration with a woman, leader of a charismatic movement of the Catholic Church, taking courageous positions on forgiveness and the unity of the human family.[3]

The Imam and the Catholic woman seem to have had nothing in common but sincere leadership of millions of people. Yet they have given rise to an original experience of interreligious dialogue between Christians and Muslims that continues to develop several years after their deaths. In order to appreciate the novelty of the experience of their spiritual friendship it is necessary to mention, at least in summary, the context in which the human family of Imam W. D. Mohammed developed.[4]

Islam in North America

The presence of Islam in the USA dates back to the colonial period and that of slavery.[5] "Estimates vary, but they [the Muslims] were at least 900,000 out of the 12.5 million Africans taken to the Americas. Among the 400,000 Africans who spent their lives enslaved in the United States, tens of thousands were Muslims."[6] Scholars estimate that as many as 30% of the African slaves (enslaved) brought to the U.S., from West and Central African Countries like Gambia and Cameroon, were Muslim. Among the difficulties they faced, were also those related to their faith.[7] An article by Dora Mekouar, "America's First Muslims Were Slaves," refers to Omar Ibn Said, a 37-year-old wealthy scholar from Senegal, who was captured and sold into slavery. "When people thought of a Muslim at that time, they thought Arab, they thought Ottoman, they thought Middle Eastern," Kayle Beydoun, an author and law professor at the University of Arkansas, says. "Enslaved Africans did not fit within that racial ethnic caricature or form." This narrow understanding of both Muslims and Africans led to the widespread belief that the two identities could not overlap and helped the erasure of Muslims African enslaved from the historical record.[8] This Islamic presence, although it did not survive, has made its contribution to the history and culture of the continent, without, however, a continuity of conscious practice.[9]

After a first immigration from Arab countries around 1875,[10] another important moment for the Muslim presence in the USA was the approval by Congress of the National Origin Act, which, starting in 1924, allowed immigration from Asia and from Muslim-majority countries, favoring the arrival of thousands of faithful of Islam. Shortly before, the movement of African Americans toward Islam had begun,[11] characterized by two processes. The first began between 1914 and 1920, when in New York the Universal Negro Improvement Association (UNIA) was born, founded by Marcus Garvey. In 1920 the organization already had one hundred thousand members divided into different sections in the world. By connecting the entire black world with Africa and its members with each other, Garvey helped Black Americans acquire an awareness of their African origins. This, for the first time, produced a feeling of solidarity between Africans and those who descended from them. Garvey coined an affectionate slogan, "One God, One Aim, One Destiny," promoting the idea of Islam as a religion of the African tradition capable of connecting non-whites against colonialism and racial oppression. (It should be mentioned that not Garvey alone but also, for example, Noble Drew Ali and the Moorish Science Temple influenced the Nation of Islam.)[12]

A second process at the origin of the movement of African Americans toward Islam is that of the great migratory flows from the poor South to the large industrial areas of the North.[13]

African American Muslims, Elijah Muhammad, and the Nation of Islam

In fact, Elijah Muhammad, father of Imam Warith Deen Mohammed, was among the protagonists of the great internal migration to the industrial centers of the North (Detroit, Chicago, and New York, particularly Harlem).[14] In 1931, he met Fard Muhammad,[15] which represented a turning point for his life and for the future of millions of African Americans. Fard, in fact, in addition to professing the Islamic faith, believed in the superiority of Black people, a concept which does not have any Qur'anic foundation. However, the impact of his ideas on young Elijah was such that in a short time the young man became Fard's most loyal follower and the most prominent member within a community called Temples of Islam, which in later times would be renamed The Lost-Found

Nation of Islam in the Wilderness of North America or, simply, the Nation of Islam.[16] Fard became not only a savior, but a "prophet," and over time he came to be considered a "god." His teachings were "supreme wisdom" to be studied and accepted without any objection.[17]

Elijah, after the mysterious disappearance of Fard, would remain the undisputed leader of the movement until his death in 1975. Elijah's message "was designed to meet all the needs of African-Americans,"[18] offering an alternative identity and a proposal to improve racial and social conditions,[19] based on the idea that "the white man is the devil."[20] From a religious point of view, however, the Nation of Islam did not possess an orthodox doctrine according to the teachings of the Prophet Muhammad. Some of the teachings of Elijah Muhammad would not be accepted by the Muslims of the East, and the Muslim leader himself was aware of this and did not hide it.[21]

Imam Warith Deen Mohammed

It is in this context that the figure of Imam Warith Deen Mohammed (born Wallace D. Muhammad), seventh child of Elijah Muhammad, is placed. It was he who succeeded his father at the helm of the Nation of Islam on February 26, 1975, when he was appointed Supreme Minister, the same title that Fard had given to his father Elijah in 1933. Wallace seemed predestined from the beginning. He was born in 1933, just three years after the founding of the Nation of Islam and, when an adult, he would change his name from Muhammad to Mohammed.[22] His education took place within the schools of the University of Islam, and he had grown up with a deep relationship with his father whom he considered a "messenger of Allah," as well as a parent. With the passage of time, this respect did not prevent Wallace from finding the courage to make known his personal point of view on a crucial issue: the alleged "divinity" of Fard and the "sacredness" with which his figure was clothed among the followers of the Nation of Islam.[23] The dispute was far from marginal; in fact, it called into question one of the founding aspects of the organization. Warith Deen, while respecting his father's work, could not accept venerating Fard, a simple man, as if he was God. His critical spirit, always encouraged by his father, would lead him, not without difficulty, to try to rectify some controversial aspects of the movement that had little to do with the

Qur'an and the Muslim tradition. Imam W. D. Mohammed himself would later say: "Probably the Qur'an had begun to influence my way of thinking."[24] Because of these differences, W. D. Mohammed also experienced on several occasions temporary expulsion from the Nation of Islam. But his commitment to bringing the organization to the knowledge and study of the true principles of Islam, to the correct observance of the Qur'an, and to following the example of the life of the prophet remained. He admitted in 1997, precisely on the occasion of his first meeting with Chiara Lubich:

> I was a person calling myself a Muslim but had to become acquainted with my own religion. I was calling myself a Muslim, but believing in something that was not Islam, and my father who taught me this and my mother who supported him so faithfully gave it to me in a way that made me believe that it was genuine, it was the whole truth. . . . But as my mind grew, my intelligence grew, my experience grew, and my heart got bigger, as a result of growing, I came to believe that . . . after calling ourselves Muslims, now we need to really learn what is Islam because

Islam is the religion of the Muslims. So, I began to study the Qur'an with an open mind for the first time, and I came to the conclusion that God is exactly what God says he is in Christianity and Islam. The Prophet Mohammed . . . says God is good, all good, and accepts only good. He doesn't accept anything bad; he accepts only good. . . . So, this went into me.[25]

As Supreme Minister, Imam Mohammed inspired a decisive change of course toward Al Islam, deciding to anchor the faith of his followers to the solid rock of Al-Islam proper.[26] In addition, he made the courageous choice to focus on the religious dimension, abandoning the political aspect of the movement. Within twenty years, Imam W. D. Mohammed succeeded in transforming a militant Black organization of clear nationalist inspiration into a Muslim community respected locally, nationally, and internationally. Probably there are three elements that allowed this breakthrough. Decisive, first of all, was his effort to incorporate more and more content of the Sunni tradition into the spirit of the community. A second element was the decision to welcome white members. Finally, the educational aspect should not be underestimated. Under the management of Imam W. D. Mohammed, in fact, the forty-one University of Islam Schools,[27] which had been founded in previous decades as an educational expression of the Nation of Islam, became Sister Clara Muhammad Schools, replacing the theology of the Nation of Islam with the teaching of Sunni thought and theology.[28] These aspects marked a clear break from the axiom "Islam is the natural law of the black man,"[29] formulated in the thirties by Fard and the imam's father. The complex but peaceful process[30] helped the community embrace the democratic principles enshrined in the US Constitution, which protect the right of the faithful of every religious tradition—and therefore also of Muslims—to practice their faith.[31]

This distancing from the Nation of Islam was also confirmed, over the years, by the different names taken by the community of those who decided to follow the imam, son of Elijah: World Community of Al-Islam in the West and American Muslim Mission. In 1997, the religious leader chose a new name for the community: Muslim American Society. After September 11, 2001, to ensure a greater sense of national belonging and not only of religious affiliation, this was changed to American Society of Muslims. The two terms that constantly emerge in the evolution of the community's name are "American" and "Muslim." Today, as their website shows, the community identifies itself as The Mosque Cares and The Ministry of W. Deen Mohammed.[32] Precisely in the effort to link this combination in a positive way—American and Muslim—lies the central nucleus of the imam's commitment in the years of his leadership.

In summary, during the three decades in which he led the community, Imam W. D. Mohammed was able to transform the originally exclusivist and clearly separatist character of the organization into an inclusivism that finds its roots in the teachings of the Sunni tradition expertly conjugated with the ideals of the American spirit.[33] In his speeches this theme became a constant motif all the way to the interpretation of the Qur'anic phrase "one community," as a divine sign that corresponds to the ideals of America as "one nation under God." The leap in perspective was evident: for Imam W. D. Mohammed, the essence of the American nation and its spirit was essentially positive and resonated with the ideals proposed by Islam, while his father had always seen

America as an evil and racism as part of its negative essence.[34] A final decidedly innovative aspect of Mohammed's role was his openness to interreligious dialogue.

> I had a desire for dialogue and friendship with people of other religions long before I began to actually look for opportunities. It was only after I had found support for it in the words of God in the Qur'an that I actually decided I would seek the opportunities for dialogue. There are many places in the Qur'an where that support is given. . . .We should not only accept to have exchange and dialogue with Jews and Christians, but as I understand the Qur'an, we are to see them as allies, allies for a better world.[35]

This attitude has encouraged community members to engage in interfaith dialogue to foster a greater knowledge of the Muslim faith by other American citizens, avoiding or minimizing the danger of fear of them.[36] The imam's efforts have received recognition of different kinds, both within the Muslim world and outside it.[37] On the occasion of the interreligious event organized in October 1999 in St. Peter's Square, in preparation for the Jubilee 2000, the African American imam was chosen as spokesman for the Muslim faithful, from among the two hundred religious leaders present. He addressed a crowd of about four hundred thousand people, speaking of the unity of the human family.

> I have devoted my life to building bridges. Inclusion was in my heart. I believe I wanted that and I think my father conditioned me to want that. That it is not to be separated, but to be with all good people. I wholeheartedly accept and embrace with you the ideal of unity, mutual sharing and love for one another.[38]

Chiara Lubich: A Life for Unity

(By Thomas Masters and Amy Uelmen)[38]

Her *New York Times* obituary described her as "one of the most influential women in the Roman Catholic Church."[39] Chiara Lubich[40] brought gifts to the world that have transformed not only the lives of Catholics, but also those of Christians from more than 350 churches and ecclesial communities, Jews, Muslims, Buddhists, Hindus, Sikhs, and thousands who do not consider themselves members of any particular religious denomination but who share the Focolare ideal of a life based on love.

The Beginnings in Trent

Born on January 22, 1920, into a working-class family in Trent, northern Italy, Chiara was the second of four children. From her mother, a traditional devout Roman Catholic, she absorbed a deep religious sensitivity. She was particularly close to her father, a Socialist, whom she described as "large of heart" and broad of mind.[41] In the economic turmoil of the late 1920s, her father lost his job, forcing the family into poverty. Chiara worked her way through school, eventually taking a job as an elementary school teacher.[42]

Because Trent provided a strategic passage through the Dolomite Mountains, the Allies bombed the city heavily during World War II. As the violence of war stripped away their possessions, relationships, and hopes, Chiara and other young women her age, many of them Third Order Franciscans like her, confronted an inescapable question: Was there an ideal worth living for, that no bomb could destroy? In response, a discovery opened before them—this ideal was God, a God who is love, whose personal love enveloped every aspect of their lives.[43]

Again and again the little group had to seek refuge in the bomb shelters; almost by chance they brought along a small book of the Gospels, which Catholics of the time generally did not read except during liturgies. Nearly sixty years later, the experience for Chiara is still vivid: "It was as if we had never read, 'Love your neighbor as yourself'—and all of a sudden we understood, ah, it's that old lady who can't run to the shelter; it's the mother struggling with her five crying children—let's help them!"[44] They began to reach out to neighbors all around—frightened children in the shelters, the hungry, the sick and the injured.

They read "Ask and you shall receive" (Lk 11:9). "We asked on behalf of the poor," Chiara recounts, "and each time we were filled with God's gifts: bread, powdered milk, jelly, wood, clothing . . . which we took to those who needed [them]."[45] Filled with wonder at God's intervention and the freedom and joy found in a life based on the gospel, they shared their stories with others, and their group expanded. In January 1944, Chiara and her friends were introduced to the one who would become the central figure in their lives. Chiara had asked a Capuchin priest to bring communion to the home of Doriana Zamboni, who had contracted an infection while they were visiting Androne, an impoverished neighborhood in Trent. As Dori recollected herself afterward, the priest asked Chiara when she thought that Jesus had suffered the most. As was commonly believed at that time, she answered that it might have been in the Garden of Olives. The priest responded, "I believe, rather, it was what He felt on the cross when He cried out, 'My God, my God, why have you forsaken me?'" When the priest left, Chiara turned to her friend and said, "If Jesus' greatest pain was his abandonment by his Father, we will choose him as our Ideal, and that is the way we will follow him." Years later Dori reflected, "From that day on, Chiara spoke to me often, in fact, constantly, of Jesus forsaken. He was *the* living personality in our lives."[46]

Like the Movement itself, the first Focolare house emerged not by design, but as a spontaneous response to particular circumstances. On May 13, 1944, from a wooded hillside where she had taken refuge with her family, Chiara watched as air raids ravaged her neighborhood and destroyed her family home. As she lay awake through the night, looking up into the darkness and watching the stars move across the sky, she realized that she could not join her family in the morning when they would flee into the mountains. She sensed that she had to remain in Trent with the friends who were counting on her, to do something for those who most resembled Jesus forsaken.[47] As she struggled with the consequences of this choice for her family, especially because they had come to rely on her salary to survive, an insight came to her not from the gospels or another religious source, but from the poet Virgil. She recounts, "Almost as if someone suggested it to me . . . *Omnia vincit amor*, love conquers all." About four in the morning, she dried her tears. She recalls, "From the moment I said that 'yes,' I sensed a new strength."[48]

Soon after, in what she describes as the most painful moment in their separation, she placed her heavy backpack on her mother's stooped shoulders. Her family trudged towards the mountains, and she turned toward the city. Many years later, the scene remained vivid in her memory: "The destruction was total: trees had been uprooted, houses were in ruins, roads were covered with debris. Tears came to my eyes . . . and I let them flow." As she wept, a frantic woman sprung out at a street corner, grabbed Chiara, and screamed, "Four of mine have died, do you understand?" She recalls, "As I consoled her I understood that I had to forget about my own grief in order to take on that of the others."[49]

She searched among the ruins for her friends and was relieved to find them all alive. Since several of their homes had been destroyed or their families had fled into the mountains, they began to live together in a small apartment that came to be known as the "Focolare" (which in Italian means "hearth") because of its warm family atmosphere.

As they continued to take refuge in the shelters, conscious that any moment could be their last, they searched the gospels for words that might express what Jesus expected most of them. When they read, "This is my commandment, that you love one another as I have loved you" (Jn 15:12), they recognized how he had loved—he gave his life. Chiara recalls gathering in a circle and making a pact: "I am ready to give my life for you; I for you, I for you; all for each one."[50]

That pact produced two outcomes. First, it generated new light and energy to understand what loving one another meant. "We are not always asked to die for one another, but we can share everything: our worries, our sorrows, our meager possessions, our spiritual riches."[51] Second, they began to discern an almost tangible living presence of Christ in the community. She notes, "We saw our lives take a qualitative leap forward. Someone came into our group, silently, an invisible Friend, giving us security, a more experiential joy, a new peace, a fullness of life, an inextinguishable light. Jesus was fulfilling his promise to us: 'Where two or three are gathered in my name, I am there among them' (Mt 18:20)."[52]

At another moment, huddled in a cellar, by candlelight they read Jesus' solemn prayer the night before he died: "That they may all be one. As you, Father, are in me and I am in you . . ." (Jn 17:21). Chiara describes that moment: "It was not an easy text to start with, but one by one those words seemed to come to life, giving us the conviction that we were born for that page of the gospel."[53] They became focused in their commitment to build unity. As Chiara remembers, "One thing was clear in our hearts: what

God wanted for us was unity. We live for the sole aim of being one with him, one with each other, and one with everyone. This marvelous vocation linked us to heaven and immersed us in the one human family. What purpose in life could be greater?"[54]

In comparison to these discoveries all other experiences of daily life faded, so much so that they almost did not realize it when the war finally ended. Within months a community of about 500—young men and women, married couples, children, the elderly, members of men's and women's religious orders, priests —had begun to order their lives through this new spirituality of unity. Throughout the 1950s, the community spent their summer holidays in the Dolomite Mountains. Each year increasing numbers of friends and others attracted by the atmosphere of unity joined them. By 1951, the "vacation" had become a small "community" (*polis*) of about 250 people of various professions and social backgrounds, a cross-section of society. Potential divisions between social groups and generations receded in the atmosphere of love. In 1957 bishops and other members of the hierarchy began to visit. By the end of the decade, thousands from all over Europe and from every continent were passing through the little summer village, learning how to live a spirituality of unity. . . .

"Apostles of Dialogue"

On the Focolare's sixtieth anniversary, December 2003, Pope John Paul II commended its members for their work as "*apostles of dialogue*, the privileged way to promote unity: dialogue within the Church, ecumenical and interreligious dialogue, dialogue with non-believers."[55]

The pope's statement explains how the Focolare's work has taken shape. While remaining faithful to their own spiritual roots, members open themselves, as Chiara has described it, "to the reality of being one human family in one Father: God."[56] As the Movement spread throughout the world, spontaneous contact among neighbors of differing Christian churches helped to sustain ecumenical dialogue. Open, trusting relationships with Buddhist, Hindu, Muslim, or Jewish friends paved the way for inter-faith dialogue.

Within a spirituality of unity, persons love when they "empty" themselves completely in order to "make themselves one" with others, so as to understand the depth of their religious experience. Chiara explains: "When we make ourselves one with the others, they can open up, reveal themselves to us, express and explain themselves, and share something of their being Jewish or Muslim or Buddhist or Christian. Some of their immense, even unexpected richness will shine in us too."[57]

This approach to dialogue has received an extraordinary welcome. Leaders of many religious traditions invited Chiara to share her experience with their communities. Nikkyo Niwano, founder of the Japanese Buddhist renewal movement *Rissho Kosei-kai*, invited her in 1981 to address 10,000 of his followers at their Golden Temple, in Tokyo. She shared the story of the Focolare's birth in the crucible of suffering during World War II, explaining the fundamental points of the way of life that had come from her discovery that God is love. She then told them, "Since in this world of ours, we often meet brothers and sisters of other faiths as well, we are living a marvelous experience. Every human being, made in the image of God, has the possibility of a certain personal relationship with him. Indeed, our human nature itself leads them exactly to this communion."[58]

Imam W. Deen Mohammed invited Chiara to the United States to demonstrate the possibility of unity that transcends boundaries of race and religion. On May 18, 1997, at Malcolm Shabazz Mosque, in Harlem, New York, she shared her Christian experience and the Focolare's mission to work for unity.

Chiara Lubich and Imam W. D. Mohammed: Together for Universal Brotherhood

By Roberto Catalano

Chiara Lubich and Imam W. D. Mohammed met for the first time on May 18, 1997, during her trip to the USA. It was a decisive meeting, which marked the beginning of a deep and intense spiritual friendship defined by many as a model for interreligious dialogue, not only between Muslims and Christians, but between people of different faiths in general. Within this relationship some key aspects can be identified: the encounter, a pact of friendship in God, and the collaboration between Muslims and Christians to contribute to universal brotherhood.

The Risk of Dialogue: Toward Encounter

The meeting of the two leaders was preceded by numerous contacts between different members of their respective movements. The first took place at a conference held in Denmark by the World Conference for Religions and Peace (today's Religions for Peace). The leaders of the Focolare[59] had the opportunity to establish a first contact with Imam W. D. Mohammed. Soon afterward, Cardinal William Keeler of Baltimore[60] would also suggest that members of the Catholic movement establish relations with the African American imam.

During his first visit to the Focolare community in Chicago, the imam confided that he had read a biography of Chiara Lubich and that he was convinced that her reflections on the unity of the human family were not only for Christians, but for everyone. Notable was the imam's assertion of his Muslim identity and that of the Muslim Society in America and his request to know if her movement had an equally clear identity. It was evident that the imam was looking for a real experience of dialogue and not for simple irenicism or syncretism.[61] In October 1996, during a visit to Rome for contacts with the Catholic world,[62] Imam

Mohammed was received by the leaders of the Focolare Movement.[63] When in the course of the conversation he learned that Lubich was planning to come to the United States, he extended an invitation to visit the mosque in Harlem.[64]

The Meeting: A Page of History

In May 1997, Chiara Lubich, a white woman and a Catholic Christian, spoke to a large crowd of African American Muslims inside the Malcolm Shabazz Mosque in Harlem. The title chosen for the event was "Unity, Diversity and Inclusion." The extraordinary meeting was unprecedented. First of all, the two leaders had never met in person and the whole organization of the event had been carried out by their closest collaborators.[65] It was, therefore, a courageous step on the part of the imam, who had proposed the invitation, but also on the part of Lubich, who had accepted it. "I could not have predicted," said John Borelli, then in charge of relations with the faithful of other religions on behalf of the United States Conference of Catholic Bishops, "how quickly this relationship, destined to embody the best of interreligious sharing, would develop; but I should have had an intuition from how rapidly the grace-filled relationship between Catholics and African American Muslims had developed since the summer of 1995."[66] William Neu, then co-director of the Focolare Movement in Chicago, admitted: "It seemed like a big risk. When Chiara entered the prayer hall of the mosque, I asked myself or, rather, I asked God: how can such a thing happen?"[67]

Imam Mohammed, in his speech, described the journey of his community toward an authentic Islam and, at the same time, emphasized the desire to collaborate in the unity of the human family.

> Islam is a religion of unity. It begins on that principle, that God is one, his creation is one whole, is a whole, that there is one universal law for all matter, for all the material things, and that everything is related, everything is related. And God has made things different, and human beings too, different, because he wants that unity to progress. The diversity is to provide the unity with legs, with wheels, with movement, so that we can have more movement and more progress. And God said that he had made us humanly different by color, by nationality to encourage

us to want to get acquainted with each other and if we get acquainted with each other, we're going to find benefit in you . . . we're going to find help in humanity.[68]

He presented the Catholic leader as a point of reference also for Muslims.

. . . Our hearts have been blessed to be here to witness the address to this gathering here in Harlem, New York, in the United States of America by a very special creation of God, this great leader of the Focolare people who is now leading also members of different religions, not only the Catholic community and the Christian community, but now she is leading even members from the Muslim community.[69]

Lubich, after briefly reflecting on the timeliness of unity in the world, traced the Christian spiritual path of her life and that of the Focolare Movement, dwelling on the experience of dialogue with people of other religious traditions.

And since the Movement was spreading all over the world, we had the same approach everywhere. We felt that wherever there was a synagogue, a mosque, or a temple, that was where we belonged.

We were convinced that we had been called to work with all of them to create universal brotherhood, basing our dialogue above all on the principles and values that we have in common.[70]

She then underlined the commonality of certain values and virtues, dwelling in particular on the Golden Rule, in the light of which the specific methodology of dialogue born of the experience of the Focolare can be explained.

We discovered, for example, that all religions teach love of neighbor, though in different ways. Benevolence and compassion, or at least non-violence, are present in many religions. And almost all of them have some version of the Golden Rule, which says: "Do not do to others what you would not have them do to you."

A writing from the ancient Islamic tradition says, "None of you is a believer until you desire for your brother or sister what you desire for yourself."[71]

She concluded her speech with words that suggested a prophetic program: "So let's hope that today will be a very significant day for us, that it marks the beginning of something totally new, a new era for us, in which we will all love one another. Let's go ahead then with confidence and hope. Let's love one another, let's work together."[72] The imam himself welcomed this reciprocity. Addressing Chiara, he affirmed:

> It's a great day for us. And let me tell you something. History is being made here in Harlem, New York, in the Malcolm Shabazz Mosque, right here in Harlem, history is being made. This great lady . . . especially you imams . . . you should know her life story. . . . God is one . . . everything is related, everything is related. . . . The diversity is to provide the unity with legs, with wheels, with movement . . . and if we get acquainted with each other, we're going to find benefit in you.[73]

At the end of the event, the awareness prevailed, shared by Muslims and Catholics, that a page of history had been written in that mosque. "This is a living story that will be told for many generations to come," someone commented. "The impact of that meeting will endure the test of time and history. We continue to build on that relationship to break barriers seen and unseen."[74]

Many of those present, and not only the leaders, had the impression that it was possible to work together, Christians and Muslims. In fact, in June 1998, Imam Mohammed participated with about forty of his associates, including numerous imams, in the meeting of Muslim friends of the Focolare that took place at the Mariapolis Center of Castel Gandolfo (Rome). On that occasion he had the opportunity to explain the reason for the relationship born with Chiara Lubich: "We believe that Allah wants us to be one people, he wants us to love each other in order to realize here on earth, as much as possible, a life in God. The spirituality of the Focolare helps us in this."[75] The following year, ninety African American Muslims participated at a similar conference, held once again in the Focolare center on the hills of the Castelli Romani. It was on the occasion of this second visit that the imam invited Chiara to return to the United States. He said, "The world must see our unity, America needs your message." Lubich returned to the U.S. in November 2000 and, on that occasion, met nearly 6,000 people, mostly African American Muslims, but also people of other faith traditions and other racial and ethnic groups, for a conference entitled *Faith Communities Together*, held on November 12, 2000, at the Convention Center in Washington, D.C. The Catholic leader concluded her speech with words of encouragement and prophecy:

> May our love continue to bring people together in unity, as it has us Christians and Muslims today . . . to give life to a new world renewed by love, a world in which all people recognize one another as sisters and brothers, children of the same Father. . . . May God embrace us all with his love. God is great![76]

Imam Mohammed's response was equally firm and sure.

> For me, all that she said was . . . "a prayer"—and a call for us not only to be good in our hearts, but to be good in our actions. We thank God again for her. And I respond to her and I see her as a leader for all of us, for all of us—I mean that! I see her as a leader for all of us.[77]

The Pact for Universal Brotherhood

The risk had found the answer in the presence in the "other" as a gift of God. Already from the first meeting at the Malcolm Shabazz Mosque in Harlem, universal brotherhood emerged as the founding feature of this experience, as Tracy Early also noted in an article that appeared the next day in the *Catholic News Service*. In fact, the American journalist defined the event as one of great importance. Early was struck by the fact that the imam and the Catholic leader had presented themselves together inside the mosque.[78] For this reason, as a seal of that day, Chiara Lubich proposed to the African American imam a pact,[79] which would seal this new friendship between them personally and between the two movements. Serenella Silvi, then co-director of the Focolare Movement in the USA, who also worked as a personal interpreter for Lubich, remembers this well.

> At the end of the program we walked out of the hall together, and suddenly she took me by my arm. "Come," she said, "I need you to translate for me." I followed her into Imam Izak-El M. Pasha's office, which Imam W. D. Mohammed had just

entered. "Imam Mohammed," she said, "Let's make a pact, in the name of the one God, to work unceasingly for peace and for unity." Imam Mohammed responded immediately. "This pact is made forever," he said. "May God be my witness that you are my sister. I am your friend and I will help you always."[80]

The pact did not have a solely personal dimension, nor was it linked only to the Muslim context and the Catholics who follow the spirituality of the Focolare. It was a gesture that meant a commitment to universal brotherhood, and its defining figures were, therefore, reciprocity and universality, as pointed out by Imam Izak-El Pasha of the Malcolm Shabazz Mosque.

> The pact made between Imam W. D. Mohammed and Chiara Lubich is not a local matter; it's a matter of international influence and resolve. We should always keep it in that true vein that these leaders represent and never should we try to make it appear as local. As I have stated, they were international in their influence and their scope for the good of all of mankind, for all people.[81]

The Italian theologian Piero Coda, present at the Malcolm Shabazz Mosque, saw in the event the realization of the wishes expressed by John Paul II in the recently published *Tertio Millennio Adveniente*:

> I think I can say that I have participated in something that transcends me from all sides. Probably the Holy Spirit has planted the seed of a new reality that we will understand—and see develop—only in time. The Pope gives great importance to the encounter between the three Abrahamic traditions, which have in common faith in the One and Only God. In the event of two days ago I seemed to see in action what such a meeting can represent.[82]

That gesture, therefore, was destined to have important and unpredictable effects.

The Consequences: Collaboration between Muslims and Christians

Over the years, a deep friendship between Christians and African American Muslims has begun and continued to develop, with exchanges of visits to mosques and Focolare centers, Muslim presentations at events promoted by Christians and vice versa, participation in interreligious dialogue at the international level. From the first moment, Lubich and the imam had encouraged Focolare members to visit mosques to get to know the African American Muslim people. Imam Mikal Saahir recalls receiving the visit of five members of the Focolare to the Islamic Center in Indianapolis and ending the evening with a meal in a Jewish deli. It was November 1997. Since then, every week, Muslims and Christians have met to eat lunch together, share experiences, and encourage each other to live their faith—now for more than twenty-five years! Not a few of the imam's followers have asked why he has invited them to collaborate with a Christian movement. And the response of the African American leader has always been clear.[83]

> Because they teach the love of Christ. We learned early on that they not only talk about it, but that, above all, they live it. This made this bond quick and all the stronger. Chiara's teachings have led us to love deeper, in a unique way—sometimes even radically. In Islam we call it "Taqwa," a state of consciousness, awareness of God.[84]

This experience of collaboration and exchange took on a more definite shape in November 2000, when, in the aforementioned event held in Washington, D.C., Lubich was invited to address an audience of thousands of African American Muslims and Catholics (most of whom were white). Before leaving for Rome, the foundress of the Focolare addressed a letter to the imam, in which she expressed with great openness what she felt in her soul.

> I am sure that Allah was pleased, seeing so many of His children, although different in origin, nation, religion, so united in Him. And who knows what blessings he has in store for all of us who have become brothers and sisters! We await the fruits that will follow and that will certainly be of great consolation.[85]

At the same time, she shared with the imam the idea of holding periodic meetings between African American Muslims and members of the Focolare in various cities of the U.S. to "get to know each other better, to love each other, to become more and more one, and to radiate our spirit to many others." As the title of this project she proposed "Encounters in the Spirit of

Universal Brotherhood," with a precise purpose: to make a spiritual journey together, following "the various points of spirituality for the union between religions (God-Love, the Will of God, Mutual Love . . .)."

In the face of these courageous proposals, Lubich stressed that it was necessary to deepen the points within the context of one's faith. Above all, "the conduct of the meeting should be thought of in unity between the two persons responsible and everything should be planned together." As for the methodology, it could be based on the "narration of experiences on both sides and projections of small films or slide-films that help the understanding of the theme." The alternation of the places where these moments of brotherhood would take place was another important aspect: "once in (or near) a mosque; once in another place at the Focolare."

Finally, these moments were not to run the risk of remaining closed in on themselves but served to "also launch some concrete common initiative in favor of the needy of one or the other party."[86] The imam's response was immediate: "I have gone over the items and feel perfectly comfortable to say they are excellent.

I too look forward to the success of our being together in the spirit of Christ Love."[87] The first of these encounters took place in San Antonio, Texas, in February 2001, and others followed regularly in New Jersey, New York, California, Washington, D.C., Illinois, Ohio, Indiana, Georgia, and Florida.

From this proposal emerge some characteristic elements of the dialogue expressed by the spirituality of communion, typical of the Focolare Movement, and at the same time of that "respectful announcement" of which both Paul VI and John Paul II had become spokesmen. They could be summed up in the faithful witness of one's faith, in reciprocity, in spiritual communion and in the commitment to a common journey that helps to deepen spirituality in accordance with the respective traditions. A few months after the start of this project, September 11 shocked the world and cast a shadow over the concrete possibility of dialogue between people of different religions. The idea of the "clash of civilizations" seemed to have taken precedence over the possibility of brotherhood. The relations established in the previous four years between African American Muslims and Catholics became an important contribution maintaining hope in the possibility of dialogue. Significant, in this regard, is the testimony offered by Imam Saahir.

> September 11, 2001 was a trying time for America and the world, yet even more difficult for the members of our Islamic Center as we received numerous threats against us, from people who did not even know us, or our community's history. It was a great relief to receive many phone calls from our brothers and sisters in the Focolare who asked to join us during our time of difficulty at our Jumah prayer service. Our brothers and sisters of the Focolare left their safe and comfortable homes to be with us on a day that also happened to be the 40th anniversary of the Focolare coming to the U.S.[88]

Effects and Fruits of Dialogue between Christians and African American Muslims

The impact of this experience has touched many and continues to influence at different levels, which we could summarize in the following points.

Experiencing God's Presence

First of all, the experience of God's presence. A Catholic couple testifies to "personal love, care and concern for us and for our family. We know that our Muslim friends are praying for us when difficult situations arise. We built this relationship on mutual love together and our meetings are really a family encounter. . . . We feel the presence of God."[89] This echoes the urging of John Paul II in Madras: "By dialogue we let God be present in our midst."[90]

Deepening of One's Faith

Secondly, it is an invitation for each one to deepen his or her faith. "The more we know each other," says a Catholic, "the more we deepen our faiths. In knowing these Muslim friends, I feel I have become a better Christian."[91] A leader of the Muslim community also acknowledges that "over the years my spiritual ascent has continued. Together, Muslims and Christians, we meet in our homes, and we share with one another passages from our Holy Books, learning how each of us lives, in our daily lives, the practices of worship and devotion."[92] Then emerges the experience of belonging to the same human family. In fact, both Muslims and Christians note, you get to share sorrows and joys. Moreover, the conversation is never superficial, but founded on the commitment to live a life dedicated to God. Diversity, both in ethnicity and in religion, is never an obstacle to believing that we are one family nor to the commitment to building a united world with the richness of this diversity.[93]

Social Consequences: Ethnic-religious Integration

There are also several social consequences. Dialogue contributes to the integration of communities and individuals. This is a fundamental aspect in the American context because it helps to eliminate attitudes of racism. In this regard, an American rabbi, involved from the beginning in this project, admits that this experience "changed my world."

> Something happened that day. I walked into the mosque and all I saw were wonderful people. They had so much light. Those few seconds were a doorway that got bigger in time. It began with one tiny miracle, that event that changed the world, my world.[94]

Particularly motivating was the experience of an African American Focolare leader, who, retracing her life, emphasized that she felt called to build bridges of unity, especially in the context of ethnic divisions, separation, and inequality.

> As an African American, I have experienced so many times in my own life how only the capacity to put yourself aside out of love for the other can move you beyond these negatives to reach out to others, to be open to them. In coming together in universal brotherhood, Christians and Muslims, Blacks and whites, I witnessed how believing in love gives us the strength to trust, to care and to become a family.[95]

The Sense of Belonging to a Single Family

Imam W. D. Mohammed and Chiara Lubich did not meet again after the great conference in Washington in November 2000. But their friendship continued and grew year after year. The two leaders did not fail to exchange letters and good wishes in joyful moments or share feelings in painful ones. On the occasion of the tenth anniversary of the historic meeting in Harlem, Imam W. D. Mohammed wrote to Lubich, who had already been ill for some time: "Dear Blessed Lady Chiara, my spirit is present for this occasion, celebrating ten years of a beautiful friendship and spiritual bonding with the Focolare."[96] The Christian leader, despite her ill health, responded, recalling the fruitful dialogue between the two movements and underlining: "We have always experienced firsthand the growing joy of being together. . . . We have shared together moments that reinforced our sense of being a real family."[97] The two leaders would be united even in the final moment of their life on earth. Chiara Lubich passed away after a long illness on March 14, 2008, and the imam, suddenly, a few months later, on September 9. Upon the death of his Christian sister he wrote: "We will continue our work of building upon the bond of faith and goodness that formed our commitment to work together."[98]

A few years have passed, and the experience of dialogue between African American Muslims and Christians, born from the spiritual friendship between Chiara Lubich and Imam W. D. Mohammad, continues. "We have tried to describe our interreligious dialogue and the best description we have found is that we are a family of believers," said Imam Ronald Shaheed, recalling Chiara Lubich in March 2014 at the Aula Magna of the Pontifical Urbaniana University. A definition confirmed, in the same chamber, by David Shaheed:

> It all started with a journey from physical slavery to freedom. But the second part of this journey, freedom for the human soul and spirit, was a grace that came from learning the lesson of love for those who oppressed us and forgiveness, thanks to this blessed woman: Chiara Lubich and the Focolare community.[99]

Conclusion: The Mysterious Action of the Spirit of God

This relationship of friendship between two leaders from such different geographical, ethnic, cultural, and religious contexts stimulates a reflection at different levels both on the different types of dialogue—dialogue of life, collaboration, and religious and theological experiences—and on the dialogical methodology. Above all, however, the universal presence of the Spirit of God emerges here with great clarity, which John Paul II had already identified on several occasions. It is worth mentioning two important passages in this regard.

> Every authentic prayer is prompted by the Holy Spirit, who is mysteriously present in every human heart. The Spirit's presence and activity affect not only the individuals but also society and history, peoples, cultures and religions.[100]

Only the action of the Spirit, in fact, can explain the encounter, the pact, and the collaboration between two religious leaders from such distant cultural, religious, and ethnic points of view and the involvement of their respective communities in an experience of dialogue that has surpassed the protagonists themselves. The imam himself said it well, at the end of a meeting between Christians and African American Muslims.

> As a young black man, in the fifties I never imagined that one day representatives of Islam might meet with Christian and Jewish representatives and other religions to discuss how to work together for the future good of all. I never dreamed that this could be achievable. Yet today it happened.[101]

Lubich was convinced that everything was born of a common inspiration from God.

> I feel very much at home with Imam Mohammed, as I do with these other leaders. Actually, I feel even more at home with Imam Mohammed because I think that the Lord has brought him especially close to us, just as the Lord brought us close to him, perhaps because of a plan of love that we will understand as we continue to collaborate and work closely together.[102]

Afterword

"This Pact is Made Forever"

The story of one group of millennials, who have experienced the fruit of the Pact in their own lives and as a result have committed themselves to working together to pass the legacy of the Harlem event to future generations

I was a teenager when Chiara Lubich was invited by Imam Warith Deen Mohammed to speak at the Malcolm Shabazz Mosque in Harlem. By the end of that year, Focolare members in every corner of the world referred to the beloved imam as "W. D." This omission of any titles—or even a last name—was a sign of deep affection, never a lack of respect for his person or the role he held.* Though

---

*   In many cultures around the world, as soon as there is a familial relationship, people take away titles when referring to or addressing a person. On learning that this is not always the case in US

I have lived in the USA since 2011, I grew up in Europe, and the Focolare spirituality has always been a huge part of my life. By 1997, I was an idealistic fifteen-year-old, convinced that a world united by peace and understanding was well within our reach, so news about the relationship between Chiara and Imam Mohammed had deep meaning for me. I wasn't alone: Across the globe, Focolare members felt an indelible connection to "W. D.'s" community. In that defining moment, we collectively embraced one another as brothers and sisters, and the pact made between our two leaders was not theirs alone; we all shared the commitment to work together unceasingly for peace and unity.

The sense of family among those who witnessed that historic moment resonates just as powerfully today. So, when it was time to commemorate twenty-five years since "The Pact" was made in Harlem, members of both communities around the United States were determined to mark the milestone in a special

culture, Focolare members now use the appropriate titles when referring to Imam Mohammed as a sign of respect. The affection remains.

way. As the preparations for the anniversary began, Imam Saahir—who wrote the foreword for this book—expressed a heartfelt desire to involve younger generations in the preparations. His intent was clear and was shared by all: to ensure that even those who weren't present in 1997 would feel that The Pact is a legacy for all of us, transcending generations.

This is how "NextNow" was born—a team of seven millennials who served as the planning committee for the events commemorating the anniversary and who later felt called to continue to work together with the goal of passing the legacy to the next generation. NextNow is made up of four Muslims—three of whom are part of a nonprofit called New Freedom Works and one of whom has been a close collaborator of the Focolare since she was a teen—and three Christians who have been involved in the Focolare Movement since their youth.

A cornerstone of NextNow's engagement is their monthly live-streamed event, "Around the Word of Life," where they reflect together on a phrase from the Bible and a translated passage of the Qur'an that shares a similar message. During this dynamic program, they and their guests share stories about living a scripture-based lifestyle as young professionals and answer each other's questions about what the respective passages mean for them. They also host two in-person events each year: one in the context of a major Focolare conference and the other in the context of the annual *Muslim Journal*'s "A Time to Be Grateful" (ATTBG) weekend. They are available as resources for both communities and are constantly seeking new ways to bear witness to "The Pact" in today's society.

Kate O'Brien

Recently the NextNow team gathered with the editors of this book to reflect on their experience together. The following is an abridged summary of the conversation.

On the experience the NextNow team had at its beginnings

When we began working together, it felt as though we were being handed a symbolic baton, passed on from the previous generation—our elders who worked tirelessly to forge the relationships that bound our communities together in the years following "The Pact." They were placing trust in us, and it was clear that this trust was coupled with a sense of urgency: They wanted to ensure that Harlem '97 would not become a mere chapter in our histories, but that The Pact would continue to be part of the very DNA of our respective communities.

In this passing of the baton, the responsibility now rested on our shoulders to explore what it meant for this new generation to work together: a generation that doesn't have Chiara Lubich offering a roadmap for our collective actions or Imam Mohammed inspiring us with words of encouragement. There was no ready-made formula; we had to discover it together. And so, the experience at the beginning was characterized by openness, vulnerability, and delicate care.

For the Focolare members in the group, it was about learning everything they could about New Freedom Works, understanding their mission, and being open to learning from their deeply spiritual practices. For the New Freedom Works team, it meant learning more about the Focolare spirituality, getting their heads around the organization's structures across the country, and being ready to learn new things about the Christian lifestyle.

Above all, it was imperative that we were all intentional about not expecting one group to simply "fit in" to the other's way of doing things: We wanted to find a new dynamic that was specific to our team.

We felt called to build a relationship of unity that reflects our generation's characteristics while honoring the work of those who came before us. This required a lot of concrete actions such as active listening, checking in with ourselves, and above all dedicating time to each other. It felt like we were building muscles—emotional muscles, spiritual muscles, but muscles all the same. And the result was always, always, always such a joyful experience.

On how the experience has worked

We have been productive! It's refreshing to be able to work on a team of people who generate ideas, strategize, execute, evaluate, and witness the ideas come to fruition. Being part of such a cohesive group is always fulfilling—but to be able to do this across diverse religious lines is really special.

In a way what we do is very simple: We come together, we talk about the work we need to do, we take the pieces apart that need to be picked apart, and we figure out the time we need to do it. Then everyone jumps in and does whatever they need to do to make it come to life. But the key to everything we do is that we prioritize relationship-building—relationships precede everything. It is from our relationship that new ideas come out, and the unity that we are building within the group is what allows us to bear witness to The Pact.

For example, when we had our last strategic planning retreat, we tried to identify what we would like to accomplish as a group, to formalize our work, and to put more structure to what we do. But we did this first and foremost to make the relationship more meaningful, not to create empty metrics or even to simply plan nice events. That being said, we know that this collaborative space feeds the relationship (among us as a team and—In shaa Allah, God willing— between our communities), makes it more profound, and continues to help us grow.

On what the pact between Imam Mohammed and Chiara Lubich means for us today

The Pact was prophetic: It was a manifestation of the breaking down of racial and religious walls. Since George Floyd's murder, there has been a new depth of intentionality about overcoming racial divisions, but twenty-five years ago people binding together on the level that our leaders were proposing was rare. And even though now there is a growing momentum to overcome barriers, it is still not the predominant way that the world operates. Not only that, but we also add the religious dimension both as a point of dialogue and as a possible solution to overcoming division. The Pact therefore remains a symbol of our ongoing efforts to break down the boundaries that would typically inhibit a shared or common work being done.

We also feel strongly that The Pact is the pathway on which our two communities walk together; it serves as the framework that we use for our work together. When The Pact was made, there was a focus on relationship-building. Over the past twenty-five years, we have truly become one family. Now we have the opportunity for both communities to move forward and engage in ever more meaningful work together. And this is precisely what we feel is our mission as the NextNow team.

On plans for the future

For starters, we want to engage more young people in this work: more young adults, more teens, more children. Our dream is that this work could incorporate the arts in various ways. For example, one of the projects we did together was the production of a video where a group of pre-teens and teens from our communities artistically reenacted The Pact. The youth involved loved the experience and the video brought a lot of joy to our communities around the country.

We also hope to continue expanding; we feel that there is no limit to how far we can bring this. We plan on engaging other communities and faith groups in this experience. It would be wonderful to learn from others about their experience of interreligious dialogue so that together we can continue to be a response to what's happening in the world. That's how The Pact first began and, if we continue like this, it will remain relevant to the times.

The task ahead is immense, but we are committed to bringing hope. Our communities have contributed to advancing the unity of the human family, but this is just the beginning. We have definitely not yet reached the goal. When we think of what's going on in the world—the political climate, the social climate, the economic climate—examples of deep and authentic dialogue are deeply needed. We believe that our interfaith experience is crucial; it is key to the hope that we want to give to the next generation.

Karen Dizon, Imam Bilal Hassan,
Mujahiddeen Mohammed,
Muslimah Muhammad, Marsha Nivins,
Kate O'Brien, Sasha Ongtengco

Appendix

"Unity in the Focolare Movement"

Chiara Lubich to Muslims gathered at the Malcolm Shabazz Mosque in Harlem, New York, May 18, 1997

I have been asked to speak about unity in the experience of the Focolare Movement. But is unity a topic of interest to me and to the Movement I represent?

Let me say at once that a better subject could not have been chosen, because the basis of the whole life of the Focolare Movement is precisely unity. Its whole goal is to bring into the world unity, which generates peace and promotes universal brotherhood. Unity is the "charism"—that is, the gift of God—that underlies all that has come to life under the name of the Focolare Movement.

But before proceeding with my talk, I would like to ask you, and all of us, too, a question: Is unity really relevant today? Everything would lead us to think just the opposite.

As each of us knows and can see for ourselves, the world today is full of conflicts. There is tension between rich countries and poor countries, tension in the Middle East and in Africa. Wars are being waged, with threats of even more conflicts, together with all the other evils characteristic of our times.

Yes, this is true. And yet, in spite of everything, quite paradoxically people today are longing for unity, and therefore, for peace. It's a sign of our times.

We can see evidence of this in the existence of so many international bodies and organizations. We also see it in places like Europe, where countries are aiming at uniting with one another.

In the area of religion, one example is the World Conference on Religion and Peace. As its name says, it seeks to unite all religions in working to promote peace.

Within Islam, we see a strong tendency towards a closer collaboration on an international level among the various components of Islam. Two of the many examples of this are the Muslim World League and the World Muslim Congress.

Within Christianity, the various churches and ecclesial communities affirm this desire for unity because they feel the need to be more united, after centuries of mutual indifference and conflicts.

Unity is underlined by the World Council of Churches and, in the Catholic Church, the documents of the Second Vatican Council continuously repeat the theme of unity. But the desire for unity is especially evident in the countless meetings that promote dialogue among different religions. This dialogue seeks to identify the common values that can be the basis for a world in the future that is more united and at peace.

In particular, more than thirty years of Islamic-Christian dialogue are leaving their mark on history. One example of this was the historic meeting of Pope John Paul II and 50,000 Muslim youth in Casablanca, Morocco (August 19, 1995)—something that would have been unthinkable just a few short years ago.

Another thing that proves that the world is moving toward unity is the existence of certain ideologies, such as communism, which no longer have the influence they once had, but nevertheless attempted to resolve the major problems of the world on a worldwide level.

The modern means of communication also foster unity, making the whole world one community, which some call "the global village."

Yes, the world is tending towards unity. And it is in this context that we should consider the Focolare Movement and its spirituality, and also our meeting today.

As you know, I am a Christian, a Catholic Christian, and therefore, the only way I can speak adequately about unity as I understand it, is to explain a few aspects of the Christian life, at least in the first part of my talk. I am prompted to do this because I want to be sincere and because I am confident that you will understand me.

Moreover, I can speak truthfully about unity only by underlining what God did to impress this idea on us. He did not focus our attention, first of all, on unity itself, but on love, which is what makes unity possible. And he did not start out by proposing mutual love, which is the foundation, the support of unity, but rather, he simply began by teaching us to love our neighbors, especially those most in need.

The Focolare Movement started in 1943, during World War II, in Trent, in northern Italy—in Europe. It began with a group of young women, which included myself. Bombs were falling night and day, forcing us to run to the nearby shelters as many as eleven times a day.

All we were able to take with us was a small book containing the Gospels, which are part of our Sacred Book, the Bible. We opened it. And something amazing happened. Those words, which we had heard so many times before, suddenly lit up for us, as if a light had been turned on beneath them. We understood them, and a force that we think came from God impelled us to put them into practice.

For example, we read: "You shall love your neighbor as yourself" (Mt 19:19). "Your neighbor." But who was our neighbor? Where was our neighbor? Our neighbor was right there beside us!

Our neighbor was that old lady who could barely drag herself to the air raid shelter when the alarm sounded. We had to love her as ourselves! Therefore, we had to help her every time we went to the shelter, supporting her between us. Our neighbors were also those five children terrified by the war, huddled around their mother. We had to take them in our arms and help her bring them back home.

Our neighbor was that invalid confined to his home, unable to get to the air raid shelters and in need of medication. To love him we had to go to see him, get the medicine he needed and take care of him.

We read: "Just as you did it to one of the least of these who are members of my family, you did it to me" (Mt 25:40). Due to the horrible circumstances of the war, there were people around us who were wounded, in need of clothes and shelter, hungry and thirsty. So, we prepared large pots of soup and distributed it to them.

Sometimes people in need would knock at our door, and we would invite them in for a meal. Around our table, there would be a poor person and one of us, a poor person and one of us.

In the Gospel, Jesus assured us: "Ask and it will be given to you" (Mt 7:7; Lk 11:9). So we would ask on behalf of the poor, and every time God showered us with all kinds of things—bread, powdered milk, jam, firewood, clothes. And we took everything to those who needed them.

One day a poor man asked for a pair of shoes size twelve. Knowing that Jesus had identified himself with the poor, one of us went into a church and asked him: "Give me a pair of shoes, size twelve, for you in that poor man." As she was leaving the church, a young woman handed her a package. She opened it and inside was a pair of shoes size twelve!

This is just one example of the thousands and thousands of episodes that occurred in the years that followed.

"Give and it will be given to you" (Lk 6:38) is what we read one day in the Gospel. So, we started giving. Once there was only one egg in the house for all of us. We gave it away just the same to someone in need. And before the morning was over, a dozen eggs arrived.

And the same happened with other things: "Give and it will be given to you." So whatever Jesus promised came true.

This experience made us even more enthusiastic about continuing along this new way of life. We told others about the things that were happening to us day after day. Many of them were struck by this and started to live the same way.

As time went on, we extended our love to everyone we met. Thus, the love for neighbor acquired certain qualities. We loved everyone without distinction (we no longer saw people as pleasant or unpleasant, white or black, Christians or Jews, and so on). Another quality was to be first to love (therefore, unselfishly, without expecting anything in return).

Meanwhile the war raged on. There was no end in sight, and we were in great danger. We could have died at any moment. We felt we had to live really well, doing God's will as fully as possible.

One day, realizing that death might be imminent, we asked ourselves: "Is there a will of God that is particularly pleasing to him? If so, that's what we want to do before we die."

In the Gospel we read this sentence of Jesus: "This is my commandment, that you love one another as I have loved you. No one has greater love than this, to lay down one's life for one's friends" (Jn 15:12–13). He called this a *new* commandment, *his* commandment. It was exactly what we were looking for!

We understood then that if, up until that moment, the teachings of the Gospel had urged us to love others, now we had to direct our attention to one another as well, loving one another in this way, to the point of being ready to die for one another.

Naturally, we weren't ordinarily asked to give up our lives; but this readiness had to be the basis of every act of love for one another. We decided to live like this. And we expressed this decision with a pact. We told one another: "I am ready to die for you." And the other: "And I for you." "I for you." "I for you." All of us for each of the others.

And from that moment on, our life changed; it took a qualitative leap ahead. We were filled with new peace, new joy, a burning desire to do good. We were filled with light.

Then a very significant event occurred. One day we were gathered together in a cellar where we had sought shelter from the danger of the bombs. We happened to open the Gospel and we found ourselves faced with Jesus' long and solemn prayer, in which he asks for the unity of all people with God and with one another.

We began to read it and we felt certain that we had been born to fulfill that prayer, that it was the "Magna Carta" of the Movement that was coming to life. But how could we bring about unity? How could we understand and reach this great goal?

We found the key in that moment in Jesus' life which for us Christians is the greatest sign of his love—that is, when he suffered on the cross for all the sins of the world, to the point of feeling forsaken by God.

And we felt urged to live as Jesus did, to imitate him by taking upon ourselves, in some way, all the sufferings of humanity.

From then on, wherever someone was suffering, wherever there were divisions or traumas, we felt that was our place, ready to bring love into divided families, to bring love between generations, to bring love among churches that are divided, to bring love where religions are in conflict, to bring love where there are tensions between those who believe in God and those who do not. And, as if by magic, we saw that unity was reestablished, with a new surge of hope, joy, and peace.

For this reason, in 1960, when we—who were Catholic Christians—came into contact with Christians of other churches, we didn't stay closed in on ourselves. We were open to them and able to establish unity with them as well, as far as was possible. Consequently, barriers that had formed between us and them down through the centuries collapsed and many misunderstandings disappeared. We decided to live, above all, everything that we had in common, as brothers and sisters who understand and love each other.

Thus, year after year Lutherans, Episcopalians, Orthodox, members of the Reformed Churches, Methodists, Baptists, and other Christians have swelled the ranks of this peaceful revolution of love.

But God's plan didn't stop there. We didn't know what God had in mind, but a variety of circumstances gradually revealed it to us. In fact, in 1977, I had to go to London to receive an award for promoting progress in religion. During the ceremony I spoke to a large audience in the Guildhall, where there were people who belonged to many different religions: Jews, Muslims, Buddhists, Hindus, and others. While I was speaking I had the impression that the presence of God, like the sun, was enveloping all those people, and I had the certainty that God was present there in a special way.

I understood then that we had to establish relationships with all of them; that this is what God wanted. Thus began our dialogues of love, life, and prayer with the faithful of other religions, and in a special way with Muslims and Jews, because of our common faith in the one God. And since the Movement was spreading all over the world, we had the same approach everywhere. We felt that wherever there was a synagogue, a mosque, or a temple, that was where we belonged.

We were convinced that we had been called to work with all of them to create universal brotherhood, basing our dialogue above all on the principles and values that we have in common.

We discovered, for example, that all religions teach love of neighbor, though in different ways. Benevolence and compassion, or at least non-violence, are present in many religions. And almost all of them have some version of the Golden Rule, which says: "Do not do to others what you would not have them do to you" (see Lk 6:31).

A writing from the ancient Islamic tradition says, "None of you is a believer until you desire for your brother or sister what you desire for yourself" (Hadith 13, Al Bukhari). . . . The Golden Rule is enough to guarantee our bond of love with every neighbor; and this kind of love would be enough to bring all humanity together into one family.

But that is not all. For example, Buddhists also have norms that are similar to the commandments of Christians and Jews, as for example, do not kill, do not lie, do not steal, do not commit impure acts, and so on. This means that we can encourage one another to live according to these commands, and by doing so, we will constantly improve the way we live our religious commitment.

And what about the great world of Islam? From our very first contacts with Muslims, we have been deeply struck by the affinity that exists between our two religions, which both trace their roots back to Abraham. For example, we share the belief in one God who is gracious and merciful, the total dedication to doing God's will, a high esteem for Jesus and for Mary, his mother.

But what immediately made us feel especially close to our Muslim brothers and sisters was the fact that we share with you a profound faith in the love of God. As the Qur'an puts it so well, he is closer to us than our jugular vein. And we are also closely united to Muslims by the practice of sincere, unselfish love for every neighbor, which all of us try to have.

All over the world there are Muslim friends of ours who are in close contact with our Movement. Among them are imams, practicing Muslims, and others who, on meeting the Movement, returned to the practice of the five pillars of Islam. Therefore, they themselves form groups that meet periodically to strengthen their bonds of friendship with one another and with us. I can honestly say that with some of these friends we really feel part of the same family.

What these Muslims do, how they live the spirit of unity, is exemplary, especially in those areas of the world where violence and racial and religious intolerance try to create an abyss between the different groups in society.

For example, in Solingen, Germany, right after the massacre caused by racist attitudes, in which a Turkish family was killed, the young Muslims and Christians of the Movement organized an initiative to promote reconciliation. In those circumstances, it was a courageous act that went totally against the common mentality. They organized a big concert for peace in the center of town, with the participation of young people of various ethnic groups who gave a witness of unity. This event gave a significant contribution to restoring peace to people's hearts. This is just one example.

We are bound together, with one heart, with tens of thousands of members of other religions. Some of them are part of our Movement; they are deeply committed to always living according to the will of God and the dictates of their conscience.

And the fruits are countless.

First of all, many, many people change their lifestyle, in the sense that they change from a life without God, or one that is mediocre, to a life that is centered on God.

The young people who live this spirit are not the immature or resentful adolescents people talk about. They become protagonists. These young people organize projects, such as collecting funds to meet people's immediate needs following a natural disaster, or activities to promote peace, or moments of prayer. Their large gatherings attract the attention of the media. In fact, a recent youth festival that took place in Rome in 1995, in which 15,000 young people participated, was broadcast on 324 national and local television networks, reaching 200 million viewers.

In families where people live this spirit, love is revitalized. The generation gap is transformed into a positive exchange of gifts. In a society that seems to be losing its sense of family values and of the value of life, the witness of these families whose lives are rooted in God encourages others to be more committed to their religious and civil life. Couples on the brink of separation or divorce find the strength to start a dialogue with each other again. And there have been thousands of adoptions-at-a-distance of children in developing countries.

This spirituality of unity, which is a communitarian spirituality because we all love one another, transforms society, including the fields of economy and work, politics, law, health, education, and the media.

In other words, this collaboration among all of us of different religions is accomplishing a great deal of good.

So, let's hope that today will be a very significant day for us, that it marks the beginning of something totally new, a new era for us, in which we will all love one another.

Let's go ahead then with confidence and hope.

Let's love one another, let's work together. A Christian saint[103] once said: "The world belongs to those who love it the most and can give the best proof of their love." And that is what we can do all together.

Response by
Imam W. D. Mohammed

We are very happy and pleased and we feel that our hearts have been blessed to be here to witness the address to this gathering here in Harlem, New York, in the United States of America, by a very special creation of God, this great leader of the Focolare people, who is now leading also members of different religions, not only the Catholic community and the Christian community, but now she is leading even members from the Muslim community.

I always believe that if we recognize good and support good, we can get nothing but good from it. And it wasn't surprising at all for me to hear that a Muslim who had benefited from association with the Focolare group and their Movement had become even a better Muslim and decided to practice the five pillars that they weren't practicing before. That's not surprising to me at all.

In fact, I have from my own experience, because I was a person calling myself a Muslim but had to become acquainted with my own religion—I was calling myself a Muslim, but believing in something that was not Islam, and my father who taught me this and my mother who supported him so faithfully gave it to me in a way that made me believe that it was genuine, it was the whole truth, and anything else that differed from it was not to be accepted. But as my mind grew, my intelligence grew, my experience grew, and my heart got bigger, as a result of growing, I came to believe that someone had given us something just to hold us for a while, but did not want us to keep it always, so after calling ourselves Muslims, now we need to really learn what is Islam because Islam is the religion of the Muslims.

So, I began to study the Qur'an with an open mind for the first time, and I came to the conclusion that God is exactly what God says he is in Christianity and Islam. The Prophet Mohammed—prayers and peace be upon him—he says God is good, all good, and accepts only good. He doesn't accept anything bad; he accepts only good. And this was a human, a human motivation in me; I was motivated because my mother told me . . . one thing she told me: "Wallace, don't lie, don't steal, don't cheat, be honest, be decent, be obedient to God." She taught me these things. So this went into me.

So, what was motivating me was the belief that I am to be good, if I am to be accepted by God, I'm to be a good person. So those things that I couldn't see as good anymore in me, I didn't like them, and I began to get rid of them one by one, and I finally saw that it wasn't good for us to not embrace the good, and appreciate the good and support the good that we find in others, whether they belong to your religion or not, whether they have your color or not, whether they have your nationality or not. If they have good that is benefiting the whole humanity, acknowledge that good, and if you have an opportunity, even support that good, encourage that good and support that good.

So this idea that is in the Focolare Movement is something that our soul, our human soul knows and our soul wants that, our souls are hungering for that and for that reason I have embraced them as my friends and I admire them greatly and I believe in their Movement, and I consider myself a person who is open to their influences, I'm not closed, I'm open to their influence.

And we know that the Christians have been the leaders since the Renaissance, the Christians of the world—their nations have been the leaders in advancing sciences, learning, and appreciation for knowledge.

And Islam now is being revived again; after going to sleep under colonial domination, Islam is being revived again. And Islam is now beginning to join . . . it's a different world we're living in. I say, and I say it often, this is the best time in the history of man, the best time in the history of man, this is a new world we're seeing now. So, you don't have too many scholars thinking narrowly or selfishly, Muslim scholars, and wanting it all for themselves, wanting this for Arab glory, or for Muslim glory. No, you have very important scientists working side by side with Christians and others, with members of the Soviet Union and others—they're all working side by side together for the better future for all people, for all humanity.

This is a new time. And so in time, we're going to see Muslims come to the forefront again, but not with any selfish plan or mission to create dominance. Because God says whoever wants dominance, he will deny them that. Allah said that. Whoever wants power or dominance, he will deny it to him. Who desires corruption or dominance, they will be denied that by God. You will think that you are succeeding, but you'll have all the props knocked out from under you and you'll find yourself helpless one day.

It's a great day for us. And let me tell you something. History is being made here in Harlem, New York, in the Malcolm Shabazz Mosque, right here in Harlem, history is being made. This great lady . . . I hope that you all will get more literature on the Focolare Movement and read about her, because you should . . . especially you imams, you leaders, even you businesspeople, all you leaders, you school-teachers, you should know her life story.

Islam is a religion of unity. It begins on that principle that God is one, his creation is one whole, is a whole, that there is one universal law for all matter, for all the material things, and that everything is related, everything is related. And God has made things different, and human beings too, different, because he wants that unity to progress. The diversity is to provide the unity with legs, with wheels, with movement, so that we can have more movement and more progress. And God said that he had made us humanly different by color, by nationality to encourage us to want to get acquainted with each other, and if we get acquainted with each other, we're going to find benefit in you . . . there's not enough; we're going to find help in humanity, in you, there's not enough. And God wants us to bring all this good help together so that our humanity will get where God wants it to go. Thank you very much, and we welcome this great lady! We welcome this great lady and we will keep her in our hearts.

Notes

1. Imam Ronald Shaheed, Speech, Urbaniana University, 20 March 2014, at the Center for Interreligious Dialogue of the Focolare Movement, in *Chiara and the World Religions: Together towards the Unity of the Human Family*, Proceedings of the Congress, Asian Trading Corporation, Bengaluru, 2017, pp. 234–235.

2. The occasion was offered by the conference *Listening to America: Encounter among Peoples, Cultures, Religions: Roads to the Future*, organized by the Pontifical Urbaniana University, 7–9 April 2014.

3. D. A. Shaheed, "Islam's Response to the American Man," in A. Trevisiol, ed., *Listening to America: Encounter among Peoples, Cultures, Religions: Roads to the Future*, Urbaniana University Press, Vatican City (2014), pp. 301–306, here p. 304.

4. Chiara Lubich and Imam W. D. Mohammed both died in 2008: Chiara on March 14 (born in 1920) and Imam Mohammed on September 9 (born in 1933).

5. See A. D. Austin, *African Muslim in Antebellum America: Transatlantic Stories and Spiritual Struggle* (London: Routledge, 1977), and A. Haley, *Roots: The Saga of an American Family* (Garden City, NJ: Doubleday & Company, 1976). For an in-depth study of the origins of the presence of Islam in North America in general and in the USA, consult J. Hammer and O. Safi, eds., *The Cambridge Companion to American Islam*, Cambridge Companions to Religion (Cambridge: Cambridge University Press, 2013); A. Zain, *Black Mecca: The African Muslims of Harlem* (Oxford: Oxford University Press, 2010) ; P. M. Barrett, *American Islam: the Struggle for the Soul of a Religion* (New York: Farrar, Straus and Giroux, 2007);

R. Dannin, *Black Pilgrimage to Islam*, (Oxford: Oxford University Press, 2002).

6. Sylviane A Diouf, "Muslims in America: A Forgotten History." Aljazeera (online) 10 February 2021.

7. Saeed Ahmed Khan, Wayne State University. https://clas.wayne.edu/news/muslims-arrived-in-america-400-years-ago-as-part-of-the-slave-trade-and-to-day-are-vastly-diverse-56104.

8. Khale Beydoun, "America's First Muslims Were Slaves." https://www.voanews.com/a/america-s-first-muslims-were-slaves/4763323.html.

9. See S. A. Diouf, *Servants of Allah: African Muslims Enslaved in the Americas* (New York: NYU Press, 1998), in particular, chapter 6, pp. 179–210; Turner, *Jazz Religion*; and S. Howell, "Laying the Groundwork for American Muslim Histories: 1865–1965," in Hammer and Safi, *The Cambridge Companion to American Islam*, pp. 42 and 46.

10. The first official mosque in North America was built at the Columbian Exposition held in Chicago in 1893. It was a replica of the mosque in the funerary complex of Sultan Qaytbay of Cairo, and its erection was intended to be a demonstration of Islam for the American public and visitors. It was dismantled at the end of the exhibition. (See Howell, "Laying the Groundwork," p. 45). It took until 1921 to see a second mosque built, the one erected in Highland Park, Michigan, by Muslim immigrants for worshippers who were American citizens. This represented an important turning point for the presence of Islam in the United States. It was built, in fact, to ensure the conscious and daily practice of the faith. (See Howell, "Laying the Groundwork," p. 45).

11. See Howell, "Laying the Groundwork," pp. 51–52. Regarding the possibility of the continuity or lack thereof

of this Islam with that examined previously of slaves from Africa, there are two perspectives that are not necessarily mutually exclusive. On the one hand, it claims an identity between today's Black Muslims and the presence of Islam within slave communities from Africa in previous centuries. The latter could be the "founding fathers and mothers" of African Americans. (See Gomez, *Black Crescent*, p. 143; Hammer and Safi, *The Cambridge Companion to American Islam*, p. 44.) On the other hand, although aware of a certain link, there is a tendency to affirm that Islam brought by African slaves has not survived, although it has left traces. (See Howell, "Laying the Groundwork," p. 46.)

12. A second element of this first process was the arrival in the United States, in 1920, of Mufti Muhammad Sadiq, a Muslim "missionary" who had the task of introducing his religion to the United States. Sadiq was the envoy of Mirza Ghulam Ahmad, the spiritual leader of the "Ahmadiyya Movement of Islam," founded in Indian Punjab with headquarters in Qadian and characterized by a strong anti-colonial and missionary drive (in Europe and the United States) to respond to the increasingly strong presence of Christian missionaries from different churches in India. (See Howell, "Laying the Groundwork," pp. 51–52). The Ahmadiyya Movement would require a separate study. For a better understanding in this regard, see Howell, "Laying the Groundwork," pp. 51–52; S. Rose Valentine, *Islam and the Ahmadiyya Jama'at: History, Belief, Practice* (New York: Columbia University Press, 2008).

13. Academic research for decades has focused on Islam coming from the first migratory flow since the passage of the 1924 law, long ignoring that of African origin motivated by the wave of internal migration of African Americans from the South to the North of the United States.

14. Elijah Poole was born in 1897 in Deepstep, Georgia, and after spending the first years of his life in the deep South, moved with his father and mother (Clara Evans) to Detroit. Here, after a few years of work of different kinds, he found himself living the drama of the Great Depression, when to escape the tragic situation of the times he turned to alcohol.

15. Fard Muhammad (c. 1877–c. 1934), often also called Wallace D. Fard, was born in New Zealand, but claimed to be originally from Mecca. He sold silk material and household items at home but was more interested in contributing to the spread of Islam. He disappeared mysteriously in 1934, leaving no trace and giving rise to various more or less imaginative interpretations.

16. In Fard, the young Poole found a leader capable of ensuring him a new existential motivation and a new religion, Islam, for which he changed his name from Elijah Poole to Elijah Karriem, later becoming Elijah Muhammad.

17. See M. Saahir, *The Honorable Elijah Muhammad: The Man Behind the Men* (Indianapolis, IN: Words Make People, 2011), pp. 57–58.

18. See ibid., pp. 58–59.

19. The Nation of Islam has made a great contribution to transforming and developing many areas of American cities, reduced to ghettos for the black population, to reducing crime, rehabilitating thousands of young criminals and finding and offering them jobs. Above all, it has ensured, as far as possible, an education system through a network of independent private schools, capable of offering school programs to thousands of young people and jobs to hundreds of teachers under the title of Universities of Islam. (See Howell, "Laying the Groundwork," p. 55).

20. At the origins of this position was an original pseudo-myth according to which such a "demon" was the

product of a scientist who had broken the harmony of humanity by enslaving Black people. Over the decades, Elijah's insistence on his mission against the white man has forced many to reflect on the social models characteristic of the United States and has produced a change in the ethical and legal spheres ensuring a significant improvement in living conditions for all American citizens. (See Howell, "Laying the Groundwork," p. 55).

21. See Abdul Basit Naeem, "Introduction," in Elijah Muhammad, *The Supreme Wisdom* (Newport News, VA: The National Newport News and Commentator, 1957), p. 4. The movement founded by Fard and Elijah has lived through decades of American racism. This is why the fundamental logic of recruitment by the Nation of Islam within the African American community rested on a simple and clear message: "Only the devil incarnate can treat human beings in this way. So why don't you support the building of our nation?" From this perspective was formed the extremist wing that found in Malcolm X (El Hajj Malik al Shabazz) its most prominent exponent with his positions of strong criticism and direct clash with the American government. In the 60s, the Nation of Islam was regarded as a powerful and threatening alternative to the pacifism of Martin Luther King, Jr. (See Shaheed, "Islam's Response to the American Man," pp. 304–305.)

22. He had done so after noticing that it was the name on his father's driver's license. Fard himself, writing a last farewell to his mother Clara, had signed himself in the same way, but above all he had always recommended to the parents to follow closely the growth of the boy.

23. See Saahir, *The Man behind the Men*, pp. 168–169.

24. S. Barboza, *American Jihad: Islam after Malcolm X* (New York: Doubleday, 1993), p. 100.

25. W. D. Mohammed, *Speech at the Malcolm Shabazz Mosque in Harlem*, 18 May 1997. According to the testimony reported by M. Saahir, it was a recurrent practice in the circles of the Nation of Islam to send to Elijah Muhammad interventions of his son which were not in line with the original teachings of the movement. In his book on four protagonists of the African American movement of Islam, Mikal Saahir reveals an interesting detail reported by another writer. A member of the Nation of Islam, a few months before Elijah died, brought to the supreme leader a recording of a sermon by Imam W. D. Mohammed that did not convey the traditional content of Elijah's message. When he heard the message that his son had prepared with great attention and ability to bring his followers to the genuine teachings of Islam, he rejoiced. His face lit up and, despite being in the final phase of the disease, he jumped up, turned red in his face and with tears in his eyes said to the various leaders of the movement, employees, and family members: "I thank Allah for my son. This is what both my wife and I have always prayed for" (Saahir, *The Man behind the Men*, pp. 182–183).

26. E. Abdul-Malik, "A Look at W. D. Mohammed," in Saahir, *The Man behind the Men*, p. 187.

27. These are primary and secondary schools, which collect classes from the first to twelfth grades, practically covering all of the mandatory schooling.

28. See A. Z. Grewal and R.D. Coolidge, "Islamic Education in the United States: Debates, Practices, and Institutions," in Hammer and Safi, *The Cambridge Companion to American Islam*, p. 246.

29. See Z. Abdullah, "American Muslims in the Contemporary World: 1965 to the Present," in Hammer and Safi, *The Cambridge Companion to American Islam*, p. 74.

30. See Shaheed, "Islam's Response to the American Man," p. 305.

31. The choices of the imam were in sharp opposition to those of another leader of the Nation of Islam, Louis Farrakhan, who in 1978 left the community to reconstitute the Nation of America, faithful to the original principles of Elijah Muhammad. Minister Louis Farrakhan is still the leader of the Nation of Islam. We do not present his profile and thought here, as they do not relate to the specific topic of this study. For a greater knowledge of his personality and his activity consult M. Gardell, *In the Name of Elijah Muhammad: Louis Farrakhan and the Nation of Islam* (Durham, NC: Duke University Press, 1996), and A. Alexander, ed., *The Farrakhan Factor: African-American Writers on Leadership, Nationhood, and Minister Louis Farrakhan* (New York: Grove Press, 1998). The relationship between Imam W. D. Mohammed and El-Hajj Malik al-Shabazz, known as Malcolm X, is different. The two were, without a doubt, very close. They had often studied Islam together and Malcolm himself described in his autobiography that his respect for Warith Deen matured in the deepening of their religion. On the occasion of the preparation of his hajj (trip to Mecca), Malcolm had spoken with a few friends and, among them, there was Imam W. D. Mohammed, who encouraged him to make the pilgrimage. To confirm all this, Malcolm, in his autobiography, admitted that he had confided to the imam his intentions and recognized the value of the advice received—learning as much as possible about his own religion—and for this reason deeply esteemed the son of Elijah Muhammad. (See Saahir, *The Man behind the Men*, p. 177.) Imam W. D. Mohammed had similar sentiments of esteem and appreciation for Malcolm X,

as evidenced by the decision to rename the mosque in Harlem (in New York City) to Masjid Malcolm Shabazz. In addition, in one of his books, Imam W. D. Mohammed spoke in detail about this friendship, pointing out that they both loved Elijah Muhammad, the Nation of Islam, and its traditions and disciplines. (See W. D. Mohammed, *The Champion We Have in Common: The Dynamic African American Soul*, Hazel Crest, IL: W.D. Ministry Publications, 2001, p. 3). There were, however, disagreements between the two leaders, especially at the level of Elijah's personal life. (See Saahir, *The Man behind the Men*, p. 178 ff.).

32. See http://www.ministryofwdeenmohammed.org/ and https://www.themosquecares.com/.

33. See his fundamental sermons of 1977, available in a collection entitled *The Birth of the American Spirit*.

34. See T. R. Yuskaev, "Muslim Public Intellectuals and Global Muslim Thought," in Hammer and Safi, *The Cambridge Companion to American Islam*, p. 276. The task of Imam W. D. Mohammed was far from easy. As he himself said in some of his speeches, motivating African Americans, Muslims and non-Muslims, to take an active part in the public life of the country always remained a difficult task. The experience of slavery was an almost indelible mark that inevitably produced a deep skepticism toward American politics and administration. Yet, the imam was convinced that without an adequate awareness of its responsibilities and commitments as citizens, there was a danger that the Black community would continue to be exploited as it had been previously.

35. W. D. Mohammed, in *Living City*, August/September 1998, p. 19.

36. Shaheed, "Islam's Response to the American Man," p. 305.

37. In April 2002 this leader of African Americans received the prestigious Gandhi King Ikeda Peace Award in the international chapel dedicated to Martin Luther King, Jr., at Morehouse College in Atlanta, Georgia. Over the years, groups have been formed for the study and deepening of the imam's sermons, both from Muslim and interreligious points of view. The imam was one of the co-chairs of Religions for Peace, the international organization that since 1970 (then under the name World Conference for Religions and Peace) has animated initiatives of dialogue in different parts of the world and has represented Islam at the World Parliament of Religions in Chicago.

38. T. Masters and A. Uelmen, *Focolare: Living a Spirituality of Unity in the United States* (Hyde Park, NY: New City Press, 2011), pp. 23–34.

39 I. Fisher, "Chiara Lubich, Who Founded Catholic Lay Group, Dies at 88," *New York Times*, March 15, 2008.

40. Her given name was Sylvia. As a member of the Franciscan Third Order, attracted by the example of St. Clare of Assisi, she took the name "Chiara." Throughout this book, we will use the familiar "Chiara," as do many biographers, interviewers, and political and ecclesiastical authorities.

41. F. Zambonini, *Chiara Lubich: A Life for Unity* (Hyde Park, NY: New City Press, 1991), p. 31.

42. Ibid., pp. 36–38.

43. C. Lubich, *Essential Writings: Spirituality, Dialogue, Culture* (Hyde Park, NY: New City Press, 2007), p. 4.

44. P. Damosso, *Il Mondo Unito di Chiara Lubich*, April 15, 2001 (Interview with Chiara Lubich on Italian television TG7) .

45. Lubich, *Essential Writings*, 5.

46. C. Lubich, *Unity and Jesus Forsaken* (Hyde Park, NY: New City Press, 1985), pp. 45–46. See C. Lubich, *The Cry of Jesus Crucified and Forsaken* (Hyde Park, NY: New City Press, 2001), p. 38; J. Gallagher, *A Woman's Work: The Story of the Focolare Movement and Its Founder* (Hyde Park, NY: New City Press, 1998), p. 37.

47. D. Zamboni, "Stars and Tears," *Living City*, 42 (2003/5), p. 10.

48. Ibid., p. 11.

49. Ibid., pp. 10–12. See Gallagher, *A Woman's Work*, pp. 35–39; Zambonini, *A Life for Unity*, pp. 43–47.

50. Lubich, *Essential Writings*, p. 6.

51. Ibid.

52. Ibid.

53. Ibid., p. 4.

54. Ibid., p. 17.

55. John Paul II, Message to Ms. Chiara Lubich on the Occasion of the 60th Anniversary of the Birth of the "Work of Mary" (Focolare Movement), December 5, 2003.

56. Lubich, *Essential Writings*, p. 18.

57. C. Lubich, "Engaging in Fruitful Dialogue," *Living City*, 35 (1996/10) pp. 10–11.

58. C. Lubich, *Incontri con l'Oriente* (Rome: Città Nuova, 1986), p. 25.

59. It was Natalia Dallapiccola, Chiara Lubich's first companion in the adventure of the founding of the Focolare, and co-director, with Enzo Fondi, of the Center for Interreligious Dialogue of the Catholic movement. Bill Neu, in those years co-director for the Focolare Movement in Chicago and the Midwest, says that he was then invited together with Paola Santostefano,

by Natalia Dallapiccola herself, to contact Imam W. D. Mohammed in Chicago.

60. Regarding the rapport of Cardinal Keeler with Imam W. D. Mohammed and his African American community, see J. Borelli, "A Remarkable Coincidence," in *Living City*, May 2012.

61. See W. Neu, in "W. D. Mohammed and Chiara Lubich: What Friendship Can Do," Paulist Fathers, Giving the Word a Voice, http://www.paulist.org/ecumenism/ wd-mohammed-and-chiara-lubich-what-friendship-can-do (accessed on 5 March 2013).

62. On October 2, 1996, the imam met Pope John Paul II at the end of an audience in St. Peter's Square and, in the following days, he had the opportunity to establish important relations both with the Pontifical Council for Interreligious Dialogue and with other organs of the Holy See. (See Borelli, "A Remarkable Coincidence.")

63. Lubich was not present due to illness.

64. See Borelli, "A Remarkable Coincidence."

65. These are Imam Izak-el Pasha of Harlem and Serenella Silvi and Mario Ciabattini, co-directors of the Focolare Movement, who were preparing the event together with the respective local communities of the two movements.

66. See Borelli, "A Remarkable Coincidence."

67. W. Neu, "W. D. Mohammed and Chiara Lubich."

68. W. D. Mohammed, "Speech at the Malcolm Shabazz Mosque," 18 May 1997.

69. Ibid.

70. C. Lubich, "Unity in the Focolare Movement, Address to Muslims at the Mosque in Harlem," New York, 18 May 1997.

71. Ibid.

72. Ibid.

73. P. Coda, *In the Malcolm X Mosque: With Chiara Lubich in the United States and Mexico* (Rome: Città Nuova, 1997), p. 22.

74. "From Harlem to Washington, the World: The Seeds are Sprouting," *Living City*, 49 (2010/5), pp. 10–11, also in Masters and Uelmen, *Focolare: Living a Spirituality of Unity in the United States*, p. 181.

75. C. Lubich, "Presentation of the Focolare Movement: The Points of the Spirituality and the Qur'an," Meeting of Muslim Friends of the Movement, Castelgandolfo (Rome), June 10, 1998. Transcript from a recorded and unpublished conversation. (AGMF)

76. C. Lubich, "A Spirituality of Unity for a Harmonious Coexistence of the Human Family," Faith Communities Together, Washington, D.C., 12 November 2000.

77. Imam W. D. Mohammed, "Comments to Chiara's Speech," Faith Communities Together, Washington, D.C., 12 November 2000.

78. See T. Early, Catholic News Service, 19 May 1997.

79. As was said during Lubich's presentation, the spirituality that comes from her experience is typically communitarian, and during her long life, Chiara often invited her closest companions and others who accepted to live this spirituality of communion to grow closer in a spiritual pact.

80. Sharry Silvi, "Such a Powerful Moment: At Chiara's Side that Day in Harlem," in *Living City*, May 2012.

81. E. Christy, "A Meeting of Global Impact: Imam Izak-El Pasha of Harlem's Malcolm Shabazz Mosque Reflects on the Significance of Chiara's Visit Fifteen Years Ago," in *Living City*, May 2012.

82. Coda, *In the Malcolm X Mosque*, p. 29.

83. See M. Saahir, "Unity and Mercy: Christians and Muslims in Dialogue: Presentation of the United States", Center for Interreligious Dialogue of the Focolare Movement, *Chiara and the Religions*, p. 170.

84. Ibid.

85. C. Lubich, Unpublished Letter to Imam W. D. Mohammad, 17 November 2000 (Mariapolis Luminosa Archives, Hyde Park, NY, USA).

86 See Ibid.

87. Quoted in "Bonding Correspondence," *Living City*, November 2008.

88. Saahir, "Unity and Mercy: Christians and Muslims in Dialogue."

89. Cited in S. Mundell, "One Pact, One People: Believers United for the Good of Humanity," *Living City*, May 2012.

90. John Paul II, "Address on the Occasion of the Meeting with the Exponents of Non-Christian Religions," Madras (India), 5 February 1986.

91. Cited in Mundell, "One Pact, One People."

92. S. Umrani, "Unity and Mercy: Christians and Muslims in Dialogue: Presentation of the United States", Center for Interreligious Dialogue of the Focolare Movement, *Chiara and the Religions*, p. 171.

93. Cited in Mundell, "One Pact, One People."

94. Ibid.

95. Ibid.

96. Quoted in "Bonding Correspondence."

97. Ibid.

98. Ibid.

99. Shaheed, "Islam's Response to the American Man," p. 306.

Notes

100. John Paul II, *Address to the Roman Curia*, 22 December 1986, n. 11.
101. Quoted in *Living City*, November 2002, pp. 18–19.
102. "Interview with Chiara Lubich," *Living City*, May 2012.
103. Saint John of the Cross.

FOCOLARE MEDIA

Enkindling the Spirit of Unity

The New City Press book you are holding in your hands is one of the many resources produced by Focolare Media, which is a ministry of the Focolare Movement in North America. The Focolare is a worldwide community of people who feel called to bring about the realization of Jesus' prayer: "That all may be one" (see John 17:21).

Focolare Media wants to be your primary resource for connecting with people, ideas, and practices that build unity. Our mission is to provide content that empowers people to grow spiritually, improve relationships, engage in dialogue, and foster collaboration within the Church and throughout society.

Visit www.focolaremedia.com to learn more about all of New City Press's books, our award-winning magazine *Living City*, videos, podcasts, events, and free resources.

NCP
NEW CITY PRESS

www.ingramcontent.com/pod-product-compliance
Lightning Source LLC
LaVergne TN
LVHW051658080426
835511LV00017B/2622